SINCE FUKUSHIMA

Publication of Wago Ryoichi's *Since Fukushima* was generously funded by a publishing subvention from the Japanese Society for the Promotion of Science (JSPS) in association with the University of Hyogo, Japan.

First published 2023 by Vagabond Press
www.vagabondpress.net

© Wago Ryoichi, Judy Halebsky & Takahashi Ayako 2023

Cover image © James Whitlow Delano 2021. Looking down on one of the numerous earthworks projects to shore up the coastline with a new sea wall, a grid which will enclose *kuromatsu* (black pine) saplings to restore the extensive pine forests wiped out by the tsunami and nuclear disaster. Namie, Fukushima Prefecture, Japan. March 6, 2021.
www.jameswhitlowdelano.com

All rights reserved. No part of this publication may be reproduced, stored in a retrieval system or transmitted in any form or by any means electronic, mechanical, photocopying or otherwise without the prior permission of the publisher. The information and views set out in this book are those of the author(s) and do not necessarily reflect the opinion of the publisher.

ISBN 978-1-925735-45-1

Wago Ryoichi

SINCE FUKUSHIMA

Translated by
Judy Halebsky & Takahashi Ayako

VAGABOND PRESS

CONTENTS

Introduction 7
Map of Fukushima Area 15

Pebbles of Poetry
    Part 1: March 16, 2011, 4:23 am – March 17, 2011, 0:24 am 19
    Part 9: March 27, 2011, 10:00 pm – 10:44 pm 27
In the Flesh of a Peach 31
A Short Life 32
Post-Fukushima Interview #6 33
Remembering Spring: Disaster Notes
    Evacuation 37
    Suffering 38
    Screening Notes 39
    Screening Time 42
    You 43
"U.S. Art Museums Cancel the Fukushima Leg of Ben Shahn's
    Traveling Exhibition in Japan" 44
Spring & Thorn 49
Thoughts of the Abandoned 52
Abandoned Fukushima 56
Ghosts 58
Abandoned Room 64
Blown by the Wind 65
12 Bottles 66
Family 68
QQQ 69
Out of Range 73
In the Morning 75
Time Passes 76

Not Implicit 77
January 1, 2021 78
January 7, 2021 80
January 10, 2021 82
January 11, 2021 84
Activism and Poetry: A Conversation with Brenda Hillman
 and Wago Ryoichi 87

Acknowledgments 101
Notes 102
Sources 106

INTRODUCTION

At 2:46 pm on March 11, 2011, a magnitude 9.0 earthquake hit off the Northeastern coast of Japan. The epicenter was approximately 128 km east of the city of Sendai in the Tōhoku region. 30-50 minutes later the first of a series of huge waves started to crash over coastal areas. The prefectures Fukushima, Miyagi, and Iwate were the hardest hit in terms of the force of the tsunami and loss of life. As of March 20, 2011, official figures counted the dead and missing in Fukushima Prefecture as 4,400. In Miyagi Prefecture, with Sendai as its biggest city, 6,100 were dead and missing. In Iwate Prefecture, where the tsunami reached 38.9 meters high, there were 6300 dead and missing (Karan, Figure 2, p.4). Over 18,000 people died across Japan. Thousands of victims were never recovered. Many were crushed or burned, but most lives were lost due to drowning. The 5.5 meter high sea wall protecting the Fukushima Daiichi Nuclear Power Plant was overrun by the scale of the tsunami. The power plant was swamped. Of the six nuclear reactors at the plant, three were so damaged that they failed and started emitting radiation that workers today, more than ten years later, are still struggling to contain. Search and rescue operations in the areas near the power plant were abandoned due to raising levels of radioactive pollution. All residents within a 20 km radius of the power plant were required to evacuate. Residents within 20-30 km of the power plant were first instructed to shelter indoors and later directed to evacuate. Residents in other areas were recommended to evacuate. In all, more than 160,000 people evacuated (Hatsuzawa and Takano, 230). The radiation exposure affected not just people but also the animals, farmlands, forests, and ocean waters. This series of tragic events is known as the 2011 Tōhoku Earthquake and Tsunami. In Japan, it is most often referred to as 3.11.

At the time of the disaster, Wago Ryoichi (1968–) was living in his hometown of Fukushima City, 80 km northwest of the Fukushima

Daiichi Nuclear Power Plant. Wago started writing poetry as an undergraduate at Fukushima University. He would photocopy his poems and hand them out to passersby at the train station. After graduation, Wago became a high school literature teacher and got his first job at a school in Minamisōma, just 30 km from the power plant. Then, he found a teaching position in Fukushima City. At the age of thirty, he published his first book, *AFTER* (1998). Prior to March 11, 2011, Wago wrote primarily experimental surrealist poems. After living through the earthquake and tsunami, he experienced what he describes as "the surrealistic in real life." Before the disaster his writing process took him from a concrete real world into a surrealist space. After 3.11, he was surrounded by the surreality of a nuclear meltdown and was at a total loss for words. In the isolation of his apartment, trying to reduce his exposure to the radiation that surrounded him, he took to Twitter to communicate with the outside world. This collection follows his writing chronologically from his first tweets to poems written ten years later that reflect on the early days of the meltdown. His poems offer an ecopoetics that, through the voices of animals and the Earth, seeks to diminish an anthopocentric perspective. Wago has gone from passing out poems to strangers at the train station to being a voice for the plight of the Fukushima region. He is celebrated throughout Japan as a keenly insightful poet whose work is a guide for how me might learn from this catastrophe and envision a way forward.

On March 16, 2011, Wago began posting updates on his Twitter feed every two or three minutes. These posts were mostly about repeated aftershocks and how the city of Fukushima was changing from moment to moment. On March 20, he noticed that his followers had reached 2263 (*Pebbles of Poetry* 65). On March 27, Wago went to a gas station and waited his turn in line. He saw others getting gas and assumed that they were leaving the area. Later he posted this tweet:

Dread. Dread of rain. From where does rain come and where does it go? Dread of rain. In the rain, the abandoned lining up

behind the abandoned.
March 27, 22:34 p.m. 2011.

In this tweet, the image of the abandoned might reference lines of abandoned cars but also most certainly has larger resonances. Many people living in Fukushima had in fact left the area, and the city's population was growing sparser by the day. Leaving home due to elevated radiation levels evoked mixed emotions. The people fled, displaced by the disaster and forced to live elsewhere. The people who stayed behind lived with the absence of those who left. Abandonment is a recurring theme throughout these poems.

Wago uses the term "abandoned," translated above from the Japanese *mujin*—literally, *no people*—in similar contexts several times in his tweets. On one level, the term describes places from which people have evacuated. On a broader level, it draws attention to the human role in human-made disasters and presents a counter to human-centered attitudes. Another sense of the word "abandoned" appears in Wago's poem "Abandoned Fukushima". This poem uses the term *dare mo inai* which translates literally as, *no one here at all*. We have translated this phrase as *abandoned* but it could also be translated as *deserted*. However, "abandoned" implies a sense of leaving something that was once desirable. There is slightly more intention to that departure with abandoned rather than deserted. A deserted town might be filled with people on the weekend, but an abandoned town implies loss.

Another consideration that translation between Japanese and English struggles to account for is the visual component of *kanji* (the Japanese readings of Chinese characters). Wago's tweet from 10:16 pm on March 27, 2011, has a particularly strong visual component with the character 人 (*hito* or person) employed for its meaning and visual impact. The character is repeated over and over again to show growing numbers of people. It is also employed in two compounds within the poem. The word 何人 (*nanibito* or a number of people, anyone) emphasizes a larger group. In the tweet, these people are walking in the falling rain. The word 無人 (*mujin* or uninhabited) brings together the characters for nothingness and person, which evokes an abandoned or uninhabited place. See the character repeated in these lines: 人人人。人人人人人。人人人人人人人。無人。風評の影。 The word *mujin*, following the visually expressive lines with growing and repeated use of the character, creates a sense of huge masses of people and their absence. This evokes not just the people displaced but also the many lives lost, and within that a sense of thousands and thousands of spirits. Below is the tweet in Japanese and our translation of it:

> 放射能の夕暮れ、私は昨日もガソリンを求めて福島市の街を歩いた。乗用車の一列。私もその列に加わる。一向に動かない。雨がそぼ降る。雨に濡れた人人が何人も歩いている。危ない、人。危ない人人。人人人。人人人人人。人人人人人人人。無人。風評の影。 (*Pebbles of Poetry* 137)

> During the radioactive sunset yesterday, I was again downtown getting gas. Cars lined up. I got into the line. We didn't move at all. A light rain was falling. People were walking around, everyone was getting wet in the rain. Be careful, people. It's dangerous, people. 100 people. 1000 people. 10000 people, 10000000000 people, souls, more people, no people. No people at all. Abandoned people. In the shadows of disinformation. March 27, 2011. 10:16 pm.

    We have translated this section using numerals to signify the immense and expanding population effected. This echoes the original text but creates a sense of counting an expanding number of people, whereas in the original text the immensity of loss is held within a single repeated character.

    In both formal and thematic ways, these poems seek to reveal the human causes of environmental destruction as well as the toll of these actions on not just human lives but animals, plants, soil, forests, oceans, and the air. The poems decenter the human experience of the catastrophe by attending to the suffering of animals and the Earth. Many of the poems investigate the relationship between humans and non-humans. The Tōhoku region is largely agricultural, with farming and fishing as the main industries. The poems "QQQ" and "Janaury 7, 2011" open the frame of the suffering caused by the disaster to include animals that were abandoned when farmers evacuated from the areas near the failed power plant. The poem "Ghosts" crosses between the living and the dead, with ghosts speaking to the living. The speaker in the poem is the soil. It reads:

>   My skin,   ,
>   even today,
>   scraped,
>   gathered,
>   dug,
>   into a hole,   ,
>   filled in here ,
>   as the ghosts of a billion mosquitoes hover over me,

In the first person voice, the poem describes a method used to lower radiation levels; the method involves digging up topsoil, packing it into large plastic bags, and moving it or burying it deeper underground. The ghosts in the poem include mosquitos, tractors, bulldozers, and shovels. In this way, the poem develops interrelationships among the speaker, the animals, the insects, and the construction site tools used in decontamination efforts. These poems address myriad harms resulting from that this disaster, not just on people but also on all inorganic material and organic beings of the region.

These poems give a voice to place. The Earth speaks, voicing an ecological perspective, showing the Earth as alive. An aspect of the voicing of place is found in the term *furasato*. Most often *furasato* is translated as "hometown," but it embodies a broad concept of home, lineage, and family that includes a connection to the physical world and the livelihood and lifestyle of the home place. It is an oversimplification to translate *furasato* as hometown or birthplace. "Homeland" carries more of the desired emotional weight but has valiances of national identity, whereas *furasato* implies a particularly intimate and local identity. Sociologist Reiko Seki explains that *furasato* encompasses the history of a place, ties with earlier generations and the raising up of new generations. It supports networks of kinship, mutual aid, and shared culture. All of this is interconnected with the land or the coastline and the lives possible in one specific place.

This connection to place is part of what Wago struggled through in his decision over whether or not to evacuate. We can see this in Wago's tweets beginning on March 16, 2011, five days after the tsunami, as the local population was learning about the rising levels of nuclear radiation. On March 16, 2011, 11:11 p.m. Wago tweeted, "My wife and son have already evacuated. My son calls me. As a father, do I have to decide?" When Wago's parents chose not to leave the area, Wago decided to stay behind and sheltered in place alone in his apartment. He stayed out of concern for his parents but also out of a strong tie to his hometown. As a public school teacher, he felt he could be of use to the community if he stayed. He was not alone in struggling with this decision. Mistrust of official information about the scale of the radiation leaks on top of rumors and conflicting reports compounded the difficulty of this choice.

In the years since 3.11, rehabilitation efforts have addressed containing nuclear contamination and rebuilding damaged or lost infrastructure. These efforts have largely overlooked the damage to social and cultural lives. Work to contain the radiation – as well as the radiation level decreasing with the passage of time – means that people have been able to return to some areas. The majority of people who have returned to these areas are older. One elementary school reopened but then closed after one year because of low enrollment (Seki, 2021). Parents do not want to expose their children to any further health risks. Older people do not want to live continuously displaced; they can return home if they accept the added risk of radiation exposure, but they find their home and the life they once lived radically changed. The qualities needed to restore previous ways of life are missing. Also absent is the younger generation so vital to a sense of community and family connection.

In a recent interview, Wago was asked how the catastrophe had changed his writing. Wago responded, "after the disaster my sense of language came to overlap with my physical experience of my surroundings" (*What Comes Out In Words* 97). This "overlap" between language and physical experience comes through in the poems as intimate connections among contradictory things, including living creatures, human-made machines, and organic elements. Much of Wago's work seeks to reveal the anthropocentrism of nuclear power and many other structures of industrial society. Wago describes his work as a "poetics of catastrophe" that encompasses gradations of rage and grief, a deep sense of place, consolation for the spirits, environmental justice, and hope. He says, "one of the purposes for me is to look for how I can communicate through poetry." Wago employs language as a way to keep the memories of Fukushima—the place, the soil, the animals, the air, the water, the people—alive.

Since the disaster, Wago has traveled extensively within Japan and internationally, sharing his writings and serving as an activist dedicated to raising awareness of environmental perils. Since 2014, he has been part of a creative group called Moving Distance, which draws attention to the devastation and ongoing recovery of the Fukushima region. He has also been a promoter of Miraino Matsuri Fukushima, a series of workshops and events that have been held since 2016 for remembrance of the Fukushima disaster and the people who were lost, offering opportunities for prayer and consolation. A number of his poems have been set to music and are performed by choirs across Japan, including one specifically dedicated to this work, the Wago Ryoichi Chorus Association.

Wago voices an urgency for action, a mourning for the destruction to all kinds of life brought by the 3.11 catastrophe, and a keen awareness that this disaster was human-made. While the earthquake, tsunami, and nuclear meltdown maimed Tōhoku, Wago's poems show us that the cause of this destruction is not unique and that many other places on Earth are at risk of experiencing similar devastation. His work attends to the destruction wrought by human activities, which begins with a first-person witness to catastrophe and grows into a sophisticated ecopoetics that decentralizes human concerns and questions key aspects of industrialization. These poems work to rebuild community and care for the emotional lives of people in distress. They widen our perception of the scale of 3.11, to include not just human injuries but broader living and ecological realms. Wago's work is vitally important to our capacity to come together to address the urgency of ecological destruction. Throughout these poems there is a compassion for the suffering not just of people in the wake of disaster but for the Earth and all of its elements.

Judy Halebsky & Takahashi Ayako

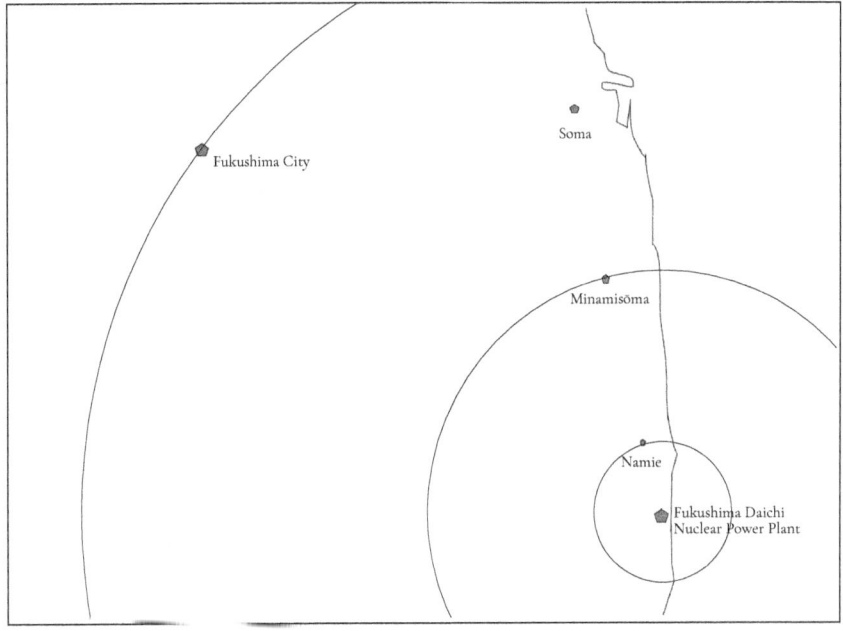

Map of the areas near the Fukushima Daiichi Nuclear Power Plant. Places named in the poems and their approximate distance from the failed reactors are as follows:
Namie, 10 km
Minamisōma, 30 km
Fukishima-city 80 km
The failed reactors are approximately 250 km north of Tokyo.

SINCE FUKUSHIMA

PEBBLES OF POETRY

Part 1: March 16, 2011, 4:23 am – March 17, 2011, 12:24 am

Such a huge catastrophe. I was staying at an evacuation center but I've now pulled myself together and returned home to work. Thank you for worrying about me and encouraging me, everyone.
March 16, 2011. 4:23 a.m.

Today, it is six days since the earthquake. My way of thinking has completely changed.
March 16, 2011. 4:29 a.m.

I finally got to a place where all I could do was cry. My plan now is to write poetry in a wild frenzy.
March 16, 2011. 4:30 a.m.

Radiation is falling. It is a quiet night.
March 16, 2011. 4:30 a.m.

This catastrophe is so painful, and for what?
March 16, 2011. 4:31 a.m.

Whatever meaning we can find in all this might come out in the aftermath. If so, what is the meaning of *aftermath*? Does this mean anything at all?
March 16, 2011. 4:33 a.m.

What does this catastrophe want to teach us? If there's nothing to learn from this, what should I believe in?
March 16, 2011. 4:34 a.m.

Radiation is falling. A quiet quiet night.
March 16, 2011. 4:35 a.m.

I was taught, "wash your hands before coming in the house." But there isn't any water for us to use.
March 16, 2011. 4:37 a.m.

Relief supplies haven't arrived in Minamisōma. I've heard that the delivery people don't want to enter the town. Please save Minamisōma.
March 16, 2011. 4:40 a.m.

For you, where do you call home? I'll never abandon this place. It's everything to me.
March 16, 2011. 4:44 a.m.

I'm worried about my family's health. They say that this amount of radiation won't affect us very soon. Is "not very soon" the opposite of "soon"?
March 16, 2011. 4:53 a.m.

Well, yes, there's clearly a border between fact and meaning. Some say that they are opposites.
March 16, 2011. 5:32 a.m.

On a hot summer day, I like to go to a beach on the Minami-sanriku coast. On that exact spot, the day before yesterday, a thousand bodies washed ashore.
March 16, 2011. 5:34 a.m.

In a quiet moment, when I try to understand the meaning of this catastrophe, when I try to see it clearly there's nothing, it's meaningless, something close to darkness, that's all.
March 16, 2011. 10:43 p.m.

Just now, while writing, I heard a rumbling underground. Felt the tremors. I held my breath, kneeled down, and scowled at everything swinging. My life or this tragedy. In the radiation, in the rain, no one but me.
March 16, 2011. 10:46 p.m.

Do you love someone? If it's possible that everything we have can be lost in an instant, then all we need to do is to find some other way not to be robbed by the world.
March 16, 2011. 10:52 p.m.

The world has repeated both its birth and death, sustained by some celestial spirit which defies all meaning.
March 16, 2011. 10:54 p.m.

My favorite high school gym is being used as a morgue for unidentified bodies. The high school nearby, too.
March 16, 2011. 10:56 p.m.

I asked my mother and father to evacuate but they couldn't stand to leave their home. "You should go," they said to me. I choose them.
March 16, 2011. 11:10 p.m.

My wife and son have already evacuated. My son calls me. As a father, do I have to decide?
March 16, 2011. 11:11 p.m.

More and more people are evacuating from this town. I know it's hard to leave. You can do it.
March 16, 2011. 11:39 p.m.

Having evacuated to a safe place, the young man, twenty-something, is looking at the monitor and crying, "Don't give up on our dear Minamisōma," he says. What's the sense of things in your hometown? Our hometown now, overcome with suffering, faces distorted by tears.
March 16, 2011. 11:48 p.m.

Again, big tremors. The aftershocks we were expecting finally came. I was wondering if I should shelter under the stairs or just open the front door. Outside, in the rain, radiation is falling.
March 16, 2011. 11:50 p.m.

The gas is on empty. Out of water, out of food, out of my mind. Alone in this apartment.
March 16, 2011. 11:53 p.m.

A long rolling tremor. Let's place our bets, do you win or do I win? This time I lost but next time, I'll come out fighting.
March 16, 2011. 11:54 p.m.

Until now, we carried on the daily lives of generation after generation, we searched for happiness, sincerity, I think.
March 16, 2011. 11:56 p.m.

My elderly neighbor gave me a box full of onions. He grew them himself. Sadly, I'm not much for onions. The box sits in the entryway, I stare at it silently. A few days ago, I was living my ordinary life.
March 16, 2011. 11:59 p.m.

12 am. Six days since the disaster. A sick joke! Six days since and for five days, I've wanted this all to be fixed.
March 17, 2011. 12:03 a.m.

In the kitchen. Cleaning up scattered, broken dishes. Aching as I put them one by one into the garbage. Me and the kitchen and the world.
March 17, 2011. 12:05 a.m.

No night no dawn.
March 17, 2011. 12:24 a.m.

PEBBLES OF POETRY

Part 9: March 27, 2011, 10:00 pm – 10:44 pm

Running out of gas, I head into Fukushima City to get more. There's a whispering in my head as I go. Nothing is going forward, time has stopped. It's still 2:46 pm on March 11.
March 27, 2011. 10:00 pm.

In the coastal town of Minamisōma. Achingly sad, an empty house and a dog left behind. Abandoned flowers that no one is here to love.
March 27, 2011. 10:04 pm.

I'm scared of the air, whatever is in the air, daunting, threatening, the air itself looks terrified.
March 27, 2011. 10:07 pm.

Almost out of gas, I head downtown. Earthquake, aftershock, tsunami, radiation, disinformation, rumors, headlines, yesterday, 20,000 people living within 20-30 km of the power station were ordered to evacuate. My heart gnawed through, I've completely lost whatever faith I had. So many shadows, rumors, lies.
March 27, 2011. 10:14 pm.

During the radioactive sunset yesterday, I was again downtown getting gas. Cars lined up. I got into the line. We didn't move at all. A light rain was falling. People were walking around, everyone was getting wet in the rain. Be careful, people. It's dangerous, people. 100 people. 1,000 people. 10,000 people, 10,000,000,000 people, souls, more people, no people. No people at all. Abandoned people. In the shadows of disinformation.
March 27, 2011. 10:16 pm.

The rain soaks my coat and now I'm wearing the contaminated rain. I see shadows of people in the front seat of a car. Rain on the windshield. The threat of radiation. In harm's way. Fukushima.
March 27, 2011. 10:18 pm.

It's still warm, the milk that was dumped just now in the fields of Iidate. The milk soaked into the ground, into the river, into this space and time into our collective mind. Brought into this world and spilled.
March 27, 2011. 10:22 pm.

Just as a voice called out to me, I noticed the menacing look of the sky. A break in the clouds over Fukushima.
March 27, 2011. 10:25 pm.

Again yesterday almost out of gas. I go downtown to get more. I pull into a line of cars. There's space but the car in front of me doesn't move, so I am not moving. I go around that car and so many others. Stunned. A line of abandoned cars.
March 27, 2011. 10:28 pm.

Well, well, yes. We're all waiting for gas to be delivered tomorrow morning, rows of abandoned cars.
March 27, 2011. 10:30 pm.

Abandoned people, abandoned cars. We are nothing, no one, standing in line politely. Crying. On Shoreline Road. Within the 20-30 km range that falls under recommended evacuation orders. The fact of evacuation orders.
March 27, 2011. 10:33 pm.

Fear. Fear of rain. Where does it come from and where does it go to? Fear of rain. The abandoned standing in the rain, the abandoned standing in line in the rain. The line ahead, standing.
March 27, 2011. 10:34 pm.

We got wet. Time stopped. It is still 2:46 pm. Abandoned dogs, abandoned flowers that no one was here to love. Minamisōma.
March 27, 2011. 10:37 pm.

In Fukushima City. A friend of mine has a radiation meter. He measures the radiation in the clothes of four of us. Of us four, mine were the lowest somehow. I carry the meter to the window and the levels go up. Radiation in Fukushima. It's real.
March 27, 2011. 10:42 pm.

An aftershock, again.
March 27, 2011. 10:44 pm.

IN THE FLESH OF A PEACH

—After a poem by Hagiwara Sakutarō

To the flesh, gathered, gathered things, memories of my hometown, a mother's love, tenderness for children, rivers, cities, skies, clouds, seas, language, houses, spoons, family albums, the tsunami, the power station meltdown, contamination zone *no entry within 20 km*, the evacuated towns, the wreckage amplified by rumors, early summer, gathering, gathering it all, the fresh, crisp, sweet, tenderness, the smell of wind and dirt, Fukushima's legacy, overflowing, overflowing things, the flesh, a hornet's rage not bitten but torn open, torn while grieving, torn while tasting, torn while praying, the peach, everything.

A SHORT LIFE

if I were allowed to return home for just two hours
what would I do?

line up the shoes in the entryway
cry in the living room
pack my grandmother's picture
try to decide which books to take with me and then give up
see if the computer turns on

stare at my reflection in the bathroom mirror
sweating and sorrowing
try to fill the tub
check if the toilet will flush
open the refrigerator
see what things in there have been kept cold

the phone   with a dial tone
think about calling my Mom and Dad

in the bedroom   lie on the futon
close my eyes   breathe radiation

wind
the crash of waves
out the window   light between clouds
everyday life

    two hours gone

POST-FUKUSHIMA INTERVIEW #6

I.

he is a museum curator
a Jōmon era scholar
and also a Shinto priest

his family home is near the ocean
in the hours directly after the earthquake
he sheltered at the museum
up in the mountains of Aizuwakamatsu

so many times   he made the long trip back
thinking about home   and the ocean

surprised to see the beach drained
as though it were hundreds of years ago
in a flash he said *the reclaimed coastline
changed into un-reclaimed land*

how should we live after the tsunami?
attend funerals?
mourn the dead?
talk to others standing in evacuation lines?

he goes back and forth to work
from the Jōmon period
to this catastrophe

2.

seeing the damage   there's an awakening   a consciousness
something like an internal implosion

cherry blossoms open   in a sudden flicker
waves crash
a voice echoes through the valley
a hunter's horn rings in the forest
a tall mast in the blue sea
and so   you start to think

   me?
   am I awake?
   this world bursting from one starting place
   everyone
   everything at a boiling point?
   am I a participant,
   party to it all?

oh yes
you are dawn itself
if you are awake
you will be born burning
billions of mornings
you
and the earth

3.

and if you aren't awake
then you will burn yourself out

becoming flame within ice
wind within wind
retribution within crime
death within death
standing on this hill
the moment petals fall
there are still stars in the sky
you're not coming back
an embryonic deer lies fallow
so you think

    to be myself and only myself
    can't I wake and go
    out into the world
    as one human being?
    just like this
    without any blessings to share or bestow
    only holding onto the turbulence at boiling point?
    you are the darkness
    tracing seasons
    petals falling
    to the bottom of what   justice?

    who are you?

    the universe

4.

while the cosmos is whispering in your ear
you're not asking for   *reconstruction*
you seek   *rehabitation*

you have declared to the ocean
it's not to *return*   but to make it *new*

such words
remind me

the rotation of the stars

Remembering Spring: Disaster Notes

EVACUATION

    March 15, 2011, Fukushima City

we could go together   why don't we
he called to ask   I thought about it
over and over   it's too hard to leave
even though later   I second guess myself

another close friend calls
I've already rented some rooms
far away from the coast
hurry   come

I hang up   what should I do
my phone keeps ringing
still we are getting huge aftershocks
should I leave

he calls again   from a faraway city
nothing is changing here
come anytime   we're waiting for you
I hang up   from Japan to Japan

***

SUFFERING

        December 10, 2011 Fukushima City

our skin is torn
worn thin
in the harsh mid-winter
decontaminated   our bark stripped

coming up from who knows where
a new skin   exposed
we are left in this cold wind

could you try to feel the ache
I want you to know what we've lost

a whole summer harvest of fruit
dumped along the shore
left to decompose

bearing witness to
wasting   withering   wailing
we are upright   the trees

***

SCREENING NOTES

November 26, 2011

*

—*entering the town of Namie within 20 km of the power station*

I am in an abandoned country
rushing to the train station

I wait a long time   no train is coming
the abandoned and I   are watching the time
confused   when a train does finally come

I think   well   where should I go
the abandoned and I look at each other
we're already too late   what time is it

rusted rail lines   birds flying
across the way   a house
with the windows left open
no one anywhere

*

—*within 20 km of the power station*

even in silence
there's a sound
called *silence*
a sound

even in grief
there's something called *grief*
a word for

even in this abandoned town
there are people here
called *no one*

even in ordinary life
there are lives
they say *abandoned*

*

—within 20 km of the power station

off the coast   in the Ukedo sea
we can see the power station's towering chimney
workers there are risking their lives   but here
it's tranquil

   in the mouth of the river   we see
   the shadows of fish   we built
   an abandoned country   upstream
   the salmon are spawning   we can't stop fate

   on the coast   just after the meltdown   people
   were ordered to evacuate   those who had drowned
   were abandoned   we weren't even allowed
   to try   to gather   their remains   we can't stop fate

surrounding our ordinary quarrels
there's an inscrutable stillness
a dreadful   mysterious silence
though we listen carefully   we can't hear

*

SCREENING TIME

    November 26, 2011

    —exiting the restricted area, a 20 km radius of the power station

screening   palms
screening   the back of my hands
screening   with my hands up
screening   with my hands down
screening   over my head
screening   the back of my head
screening   the sole of my left shoe
screening   the sole of my right shoe
screening   my entire body

screening   what is outer space
screening   what is a hometown
screening   what is life
screening   what is radiation
to us
what is most precious
what   cannot be measured

***

YOU

(no date)

precious
you

what are you
doing now

you are me
I am you

from the obsidian depths of night
it's you I am thinking about

and for me
from me

you
I won't give up on

for you
I won't give up

"US ART MUSEUMS CANCEL THE FUKUSHIMA LEG OF BEN SHAHN'S TRAVELING EXHIBITION IN JAPAN"

dear Ben Shahn
what are you thinking

your artwork
hasn't arrived in Fukushima
I'm disappointed

dear Ben Shahn
what could you be thinking
it's a shame   isn't it

"U.S. Art Museums Concerned About Radiation Levels In Fukushima"

seven U.S. Art Museums
cancel plans
to exhibit 69 works
in Fukushima

so disturbing
my fingers tremble
I can't even type

dear Ben Shahn
have you lost your nerve
we live with such fear
it kills
even art

I was planning
to see your work again
this coming July
at the Fukushima Prefecture Art Museum

last December
at the Hayama Art Museum
as promised
I looked deep into your soul
saw you unblemished
each drawing one after the other
I promised that we'd meet again
but the walls are bare

did you betray us
did your drawings betray us
did your future-self betray us

isn't it terrible
Ben Shahn

no
Ben Shahn
it's not your fault
but
why won't
these drawing
be shown in Fukushima

Ben Shahn
you catch the absurdity
of the human world

with eyes
and brush stroke
and line
and color
and breathe
and justice
and energy
and life
and vision
and discrimination
and prejudice
and violence
and devastation
and evidence
and nuclear tests
and nonfiction
and bombings
and obliterated city skylines
and the children playing there
and their vision
and their innocence
and their spirit
that's what we need most right now
for Fukushima
for everyone
why cancel now
what has betrayed us
and the guilt
who created it
who carries it
who denies it

Ben Shahn
are you looking
away

does the wind betray us
does the sky betray us
does the sea betray us
do the clouds betray us
drowned by Ben Shahn
the wind
the sky
the sea
the clouds
the people
the cities
the love
the fierceness
the grief
the heart
the tenderness
the lives
the justice
the sincerity
in how children part their hair
wind through a back alley
why break your promise

for us here in Fukushima
why isn't
all of *Ben Shahn* given to us
in this world

does art exist
does justice exist
do we exist
so much loss
Ben Shahn, don't look away

SPRING & THORN

—Based on Sakutarou Hagiwara's poem, "Sentimental Hands"

anyone would be at a loss about what to do with a thorn in their fingertip
without hesitation I welcome a faux solar eclipse in my body
all of a sudden a solid dark shadow follows another dark shadow
this is the time a pebble in spring is kicked by a pebble in spring
and a butterfly is blamed   this is the time   I desperately coax my
internal organs   to continue to walk   this is the time
oh, the shadow of a bird chasing a bird that continues to smile
over there in the marsh is a sea we've never looked for

worrying about the thorn in my fingertip   I breathe slowly
the blade sharpens as I watch the knife
because yesterday the very top of the walnut tree was hacked apart
because the day before yesterday clouds threatened to open
because the night before that a wild cat's dream burst open
from within a finger

so now   I am climbing a hill   little by little   sore as I go up
or I'm not so sore   I let my thoughts smooth the thorn in my fingertip
not sure of what to do   going down a slight hill   I see branches falling
picking them up and gathering them   I can hear a dog barking
crape myrtle withering in a green field
the tree   the shadow and the wind   my gut remembers

the thorn in my fingertip slowly numbs   the thorn
and then my finger goes numb   the thorn and my finger
I'm here but not here   even with the sharp pain in my fingertip

I don't flinch   not even a little bit sore   I am in the fairly dreadful
present but   I am also a personification past tranquility

I am alive here while inside my finger
there are yellow pistons standing straight up promising never to break
within the person I am today   the universe continues to sharpen
the unknown wields its meaning   completely illegible
the state highway bends further and further away
a little bright yellow finger stands straight within my index finger

a shoal of fish breaks up   without knowing why the blue sky is so calm
with one leg a skylark hops on a windless tomorrow
the swirl of my fingerprints calls up the far back Jōmon era
in my finger there's a yellow ball-point pen and an answer sheet marked o

while all this ensues   a swarm of this spring's tiny shrimp turn pink
how do my cousins remember that day years ago   in our school's
cloakroom   teasing back and forth   chasing each other's shadows

billons of them under our feet
an eyepatch reflects back to me the mist and the tsunami
while finally a lovely peacock approaches
if we could cry for the spring leaves opening against all the wreckage
there would be no summer rebellion
the world sits in an empty swing   while the abandoned push her back
and forth I can't do anything about the rust on the iron gate of the
abandoned city hall   because it's noon in the backyard in my finger where
there's a yellow persimmon tree
because there's still a yellow electricity pole in my finger

by the way   what should I do with the thorn
I can't yank it out   there's a severe lack of pain

or the horror of fingers numb to the pain
I know this matters
so I better not pull it out

oh, the freshness of these hills in spring
as I climb   the thorn in my finger sharpens
signal of a new beginning
because I worry about the thorn in my finger obsessively
my shadow stretches down the length of the hill
and becomes a new thorn within my soul
pull it out or don't pull it out

my damaged fingertip peaks out
on the hill I hold my breath and follow a butterfly   fresh from her cocoon
the cruel demon of spring
casts a spell of sunshine through the clouds

amazed by a small pair of wings over the spring mountains catching
the light   a sharp wind cuts into my thoughts
for those I love
this might be a good omen   the buds of spring

THOUGHTS OF THE ABANDONED

dark dark   a pitch-dark night without any moon

    on the other side   of a burned globe
    there are murmuring oceans   power stations   and the dark
    on the other side   of a paper mâché earth   there's an abandoned town
    paa paa   it's a pitch-dark night without any moon

nothing but spinning round and round   darkness seeks darkness
this time, the darkness is spinning the earth   while the abandoned
wander in the dark   cows   dogs   horses   cats   people
a pheasant with her sharp high-pitched cry   is calling

    darkness   rejects the night
    still working   on a metaphor for death
    this perception of time   right now   throw a wrench
    into the plutonium   terror   madness   realms of hell

one minute late   the dark doesn't buy into the dream   of a self-sustaining
nuclear chain reaction   becoming the dark   the water bug snickers
trying not to laugh   in the dark   becoming the dark   calling up their
memories   of being abandoned   houses   dogs   cats   sandals   bicycles

    the darkness won't give in to darkness   today somewhere
    bickering begins   screaming continues   this town
    this windless shoreline   tries to go on after being abandoned
    an electric pole asks itself   *what should I do now?*

in the dark   a village of pheasants collapses again indifferently
after eating well all season   the pheasants were shot one by one

long finger bent around the trigger   the abandoned shrug their shoulders
the birds should have cried   *dark dark*   a pitch-dark night without any moon

    in the darkness   a whaling ship crosses the night
    at the very bottom of the hull   a camel collapsed and died
    and wasn't ever born   its soul reincarnated into a novice pitcher
    his fist clenching a baseball   asking *what should I do now?*   *dark dark*
    a pitch-dark night without any moon

dark clouds cover the fireflies   exposing them to black rain   full of radiation
grief grieves for grief   anger gets angry with anger   despair abuses despair
a magnet shattered to bits   somewhere in the dark
a little sparrow bites at the pieces
dark dark   a pitch-dark night without any moon

in the darkness   a globe is spinning   from shadow to shadow
from the earth's interior   to the Milky Way   governed by the rules of rotation
does the earth understand these limits   *dark dark*   a pitch-dark night
without any moon   the power plant goes ahead resuming operations

do you know salmon jump in the darkness   carrying their eggs up river to spawn
do you know   how they live forever   how they die in spring
dark dark   a pitch-dark night without any moon   a hundred million tiny eggs
buried in the belly of the earth   they will all be forgotten

    at night   I can't sleep thinking about who to blame
    the power within an atom   continues spinning
    within even the smallest crustacean   on the other side of the world
    in a house in a small village near a window   *dark dark*
    without any moon   a reporter offers a cheap critique, takes a piss,
    and sleeps soundly

to cite the collapse of a village of pheasants
there's no mistaking it   I become an allegory of myself
to say it another way   you are your own personification
surely, the world is a metaphor for the world

    the bus with the stuffed pheasants and the abandoned people continues
    forward   into the darkness   which reveals nothing but the bleak
    desperation   of the world we keep running toward
    filled with the thoughts of the abandoned

the calm of the darkness doesn't diminish the silence
only the fear in the voices that stayed behind
if I ask the darkness for evidence   the darkness, absolute darkness
answers with nothing   nothing but a terrified silence
within all the talking and chatter

    completely unexpectedly the darkness wakes up
    in dark from the dark   she lifts her face and continues pulling out
    a back molar   I think that's the *Lotus Sutra*
    playing over the PA system of this abandoned town

waking up   astonished by the endless darkness
all kinds of people quietly forming an orderly line
no one breaks the rules
this line of the abandoned goes on and on

    while everything's still hiding within the darkness
    arrrrr the darkness moans
    and continues to berate itself
    the footsteps of the abandoned are surrounded by darkness

it's forbidden to follow them   not even a little bit
what to do about the ant crawling inside my ear
everything is still hiding within the darkness
darkness doesn't know the darkness   for the adandoned   it's futile
nothing comes from their   innocence or selflessness

>
> *dark dark*   a pitch-dark night without any moon
> the darkness is afraid of the darkness   the darkness atones for the
> darkness   the darkness scoffs at the darkness   and when the
> darkness becomes the darkness does the darkness do nothing but
> climb the shadowed north slope

standing in line
how far does it stretch   the abandoned in line with their eyes open
oh   they can also screen the darkness for toxins
dark dark   a pitch-dark night without any moon

>
>
> *dark dark*   a pitch-dark night without any moon
> that sounds like the *Lotus Sutra*
> playing over the PA system of this abandoned town
> *dark dark*   a pitch-dark night without any moon

ABANDONED FUKUSHIMA

abandoned Fukushima on this hushed rainy night
within the hush   there is a tenderness
a cold wind jostles a swing in the city park
pushing the rusty chains back and forth

abandoned Fukushima on this hushed rainy night
within the hush   my mother carries a deep compassion
as she rushes through the wet streets
the small marshes are silent in falling rain

abandoned Fukushima on this hushed rainy night
within the hush   a husky sigh as a boy drifts off to sleep
on the back of his eyelids   he sees wild horses in a Tibetan field
at the neighbor's house   camellias are falling in a rush

abandoned Fukushima on this hushed rainy night
within the hush   in the freezing cold   there is the first draft of a poem
with promises whirling on am empty page
in the next town   the vending machines are all sold out

abandoned Fukushima on this hushed rainy night
within the hush   who cries
remembering those who have left this world
keeping their memory alive
an ocean rests on these eyelids

abandoned Fukushima on this hushed rainy night   a small train station
a forsaken ticket gate   a pristine train waiting to depart

on the midnight platform
what could be footsteps pass

abandoned Fukushima on this hushed rainy night   a river flows
birds are talking about their exploits in the sky
they spread their wings over the spinning earth
could it be that our dreams are about to start

so hushed this rainy night
our souls sleep in the darkness

hushed rain and a glimmering dawn   the rain stops
hush *hushed*   fallen over by light
morning breaks with an infant's first cry
and suddenly   I become a parent
these arms cradling the baby

passed down to me

   oh, child with eyes open
   your journey through the rainy night
   oh, child of Fukushima
   born anew

thank you for arising into the world

this is your dawn

GHOSTS

    The ghosts of mosquitoes
        wander withered fields
   seeking our salty skin
,
                          , swarming my head

I cannot see their shape at all   and we
        ,   have no idea where to scratch
,
.
         ,,

a shovel left on the small of my back,
           what should I do with it?
       ,   the tracks left by bulldozers ,
    landfill,
   ,   to dump a hole within a hole
 ,
   My skin,   ,
     even today,
       scraped,
        gathered,
         dug,
,   into a hole,   ,
                filled in here ,
as the ghosts of a billion mosquitoes hover over me,
        ,
     somewhere, I'm itchy ,
       ragged top soil
the only thing we can do today is dig, bury the soil
                              hole by hole

there's no other choice
 without fail, the sun rises and even within this landfill, morning dawns
in this hole lightning strikes
in the field footprints without a body
keep going
           dead trees stand   bark stripped bare
,,   .

because a division of invisible mosquitoes
,   can't shake the hair
,   that has grown on the electric pole
,   we live in total darkness

under
a light bulb where someone has filched the filament
,
trembling in the darkness until yesterday we could see a future
continuing to sprinkle salt
                            on sliced bacon, slightly burned
                                                    thinking of
salt and pepper, snow in a field
            an electric pole grows a mustache
                    ,   too scared to draw close
                                                    and the
ghosts have no legs
                        absurd, of course, how they make waves
in the swimming pool across town
even in the midday light
                                                ,   .

the ghosts of the mountains,   ,

                                        the ghosts of rain puddles
                         the ghosts of cows,
    the ghosts of birds,
                today, here in Japan,
                wandering among us   ,

            the elephant was famished enough to eat matches
                    she tries to hide the smoke billowing from of her trunk
walking through the market place   everyone knows
                                        the lashings she bears
                    undrawn and abandoned, the well murmurs
                        a salamander then a lizard on its steep walls

from the worn edges of winter cloth   ,
          ,   from some far off season   ,
          ,   millions of trucks
          ,   haul our sweaty, salty skin
as in a Franz Kafka dream
endless profusion of mosquitoes transformed back into larvae in the landfill ,
three trucks carry   ,
          ,   cotton gloves missing fingers
          ,,,,,   they try to carry them
                , to a secret hole in the ground

buried   ,
there
                            ,   ,
calcified beside our imagination and no longer breathing ,
 ,   buried
heads of cabbage left in the fields, rotting ,
buried   ,
the deep violet scud missile station   ,
buried ,

        the causes of all this
        buried
           in the sand at the beach
in a dazed twilight
        I used up 18 colored pencils
            trying to dye the world
                      the ghost of
a dragonfly becomes a queen bee in winter

        death
           becomes a meaningless well
,   an absolute night
                as high black weeds gust
back and forth
        in the full moon's terror
                the mind does not cease its careful
deliberations   in the brilliant dawn   the ghosts of mosquitoes
            relentlessly attack the dirt of this withered fie
ld

what should I do with the ghosts of cranes?
            with the ghosts of bulldozers?
                with the ghosts of plastic
tarps?
                the ghosts of persimmons that
have ceased ripening
        the ghosts of the bicycle peddles
        that have had their bodies stolen

                and so

        the only choice is to dig further holes

why?

it's obvious
here in Japan
there's no land left to dig
and so
the only thing to do is dig
why?
it's obvious

but still

here in Japan

        the only choice is to bury the soil
        why?
it's obvious

here in Japan
because there's no space left to bury anything
and so
the only thing to do is to keep burying
why?

it's obvious
    what space

    what hole

what for
for digging holes

   there's no open space to bury anything
   the only thing left to do is to bury
   why?
   it's obvious

            dig here

   why?

   bury here
   why?

  because bare trees are standing

    ghosts of mosquitoes brush my ears

these ghosts will be looking to prick our salty skin
              forever
           the ground
        shining
    but *ahhhhh*

in this abandoned countryside
from this untouched well
desire springs back thick and bursting

ABANDONED ROOMS

some towns were left like this   one day
every room deserted
with no hope of newcomers
closed and shuttered   room after room left

in the humidity   moldering
we can't keep on like this
someone needs to open the windows   clean up a little
but no one cares

the stagnant air is getting thicker and thicker
sometimes a mouse gets in   chews on the wood
and leaves a trail

could we at least open the windows
fumbling hands on the latch   it opens
but right away   the next house locks itself   this town
remains   like this   it continues   deserted rooms

town of shuttered windows
isn't it a basic human   action
to open   the windows

BLOWN BY THE WIND

on that one day
certain words disappeared completely
in my backyard   even now
words tunnel within words
soil is buried within the soil
from word to word   from dirt to dirt
to the power lines   I mutter
no one knows how to dig dirt out of dirt
blown as they are by the wind
blown as they've been by the wind

12 BOTTLES

our drinking water comes from a dam in the mountains
since the meltdown   the radioactive gunk has settled to the bottom
and supposedly   won't mix with the water on top

it's safe   the officials tell us again
people have their doubts
it's best to avoid a large-scale decontamination   they say
which would stir up the dam and raise the contaminants

an old couple   evacuated to a small apartment
want to spend their last years in their house
but they worry about the water

*

permitted to return to their house   they do not use the water there

*

but travel to the kitchen sink   in the evacuee apartment
on the third floor

up and down three flights of stairs   it's hard for them

they fill 2-liter bottles   12 for drinking

for washing face and hands   for cooking rice

to live like water
    after one or two days   the bottles are empty and they travel back

to the faucet   40 km away

FAMILY

today after such a long time away   I returned home
I couldn't believe it   raccoons   in the ceiling
three of them ambling around
so frustrating

today after such a long time away   I returned home
and discovered a gang of rats hanging out
the stuffed Mickey Mouse in my son's room
gnawed and torn   miserable

today after such a long time away   I returned home
things had been stolen from the house
in the garden   grasses grown over the fence   people
how do we make it?

    today after such a long time away   I returned home
    in the ceiling   my wife   my son
    and me walking around
    shacking up with the raccoons

Q Q Q

starving cow, do you walk slowly?
starving cow, do you walk with your feet firmly on the ground?
starving cow, do you walk over ordinary grass?
first with the right foot, then with the right foot, then with the right?
is there something you want to know?
what is the meaning of eating grass?
wind and dirt and sun, where are you going?
do you think you'll follow?
what does it mean to eat this living grass?
from the grass, will your belly learn this geography?
what do you mean by conjuring your shadow?
what do you mean letting the grasshopper bring you happiness?
do those endless six bare feet search for a drunken finish line?
on a Sunday could you become a bright green long horned grasshopper?
does the tricycle your brother ditched on the street fall over?
starving cow, are you growing a mustache only on your shadow?
will you wander the streets of Pisa someday?
will you ask your fellow black cows about it?
what does it mean to spend life ruminating and ruminating?
what does it mean to slowly grow horns?
first with the right foot, then with the right foot, then with the right?
why continue standing here in the dirt while wasting away?
can the cow's inner intense calm keep expanding?
blown over for no reason?
what does it mean, the electric wires buzzing?
does a bird, speckled with white, harvest mint leaves?
in the aching wooden cows, what future do you see?
what do you mean the rain puddles in your head reflect a blue sky?
oh, do the shadows of cows fall in a line?

here on the ground are their black shapes standing together?
does the wind walk?
what of the cast off tractor?
does it carry ragged grasses?
to the abandoned farm?
did only one bird feather fall?
can a cloud's ear hear it?
first with the right foot, then with the right foot, then with the right?
in the whole world is there any place that doesn't need a power supply?
first with the left foot, then with the left foot, then with the left?
must we use the earth as a power supply?
first with the right foot, then with the right foot, then with a hand?
are the voices over our heads murmuring in harmony with the voices over our heads?
am I not allowed to be myself?
because compromise appears as a thunderstorm?
hiding under a rock, the lizard's gemstone eyes?
can you see the piles of discarded ladders and gloves?
does the eagle's shadow shoo away the baker's ghost?
the cow's eyes swollen from crying?
the gritty months worn by sandpaper?
like a rough season filed down?
precious water sleeting from the cow's eyes?
footprints through the salty mud drinking back up to the cow's eyes?
for white? for red?
for blue? for orange?
for light green? for peach?
the black of betrayal in the cow's eyes?
do they live at full throttle? do they burn through this life?
is the universe hidden inside a black button-sized candy in the cow's eye, glimmering?
these eyes?

within the saliva, is the saliva damp?
within the hoof, is the hoof fleeing?
when a cow steps on its shadow, do its legs sink into the earth?
ploddingly but a pinch faster, the cow is eating a cloud?
ever so slightly, does the cow scratch the sand, kick the ground, and hush the rain?
first with the left & right feet, then with the left & right feet, and then, not even trying?
does the abandoned cow, still today, believe in the beauty of nature?
who is thinking about the abandoned cow?
eating two or three bites, jaw slowly grinding?
underneath the straw hat, are horns moving at all?
ah, since that day, is anyone thinking of us?
cows left here to wander aimlessly?
is no one going to raise us?
in the breaking rain?
legs sprouting out of ears, sprouting out of the rump, sprouting out of forearms?
legs sprouting out of the liver, the colon, the spleen?
legs sprouting out of the sky, out of pastures, out of clock towers?
legs sprouting out of Siberia, out of the Straits of Dover, out of the Yellow River?
legs sprouting out of legs, sprouting out of legs, sprouting out of legs?
legs sprouting out out sprouting out out sprouting out out ?
legs sprouting out of legs out of legs out of legs?
legs out of sprouting out of sprouting out of sprouting?
do you see?
are we just this herd?
are we clinging to this squandered soil?
are we merely chewing our cud?
are we becoming the landscape?
are we becoming a question?
in the shape of a cow?
a ranch?
politely?

trying to answer?
while starving?
this?
what is it about?
what does it mean to speak gently?
what about having two strong hands?
what about having two solemn horns?
what about being honest but salivating?

does the starving cow know how to stomp gravely?
does that starving cow walk on ordinary grass?

OUT OF RANGE

December 21, 2015:

a man asks the person beside him   have you heard the policy
"decontamination efforts will not extend to forests beyond the living range"

what does within   "the living range"   mean
what does beyond   "the living range"   mean
wild boars and all sorts of other animals are moving
beyond their   "living range"   into our   "living range"
are these animals in   "the animal range"

December 23, 2015:

another man whispers
"if the Takahama nuclear power plant is allowed to restart
it could generate fuel within a day"
"beyond the range of daily living"   does not mean   "decontaminated"
but does   "within the living range"   mean   "restart"

another man interrupts
"so, wild boars are under the jurisdiction of the Ministry of Health
domestic pigs are under the jurisdiction of the Ministry of Agriculture
what about the boar-pigs   when wild boars and pigs interbreed
which administration is in charge of that"

another man asks   about the possibility
of a ninth planet in our solar system

after that   they talk seriously and casually   sometimes arguing
sometimes resting their hands on each other's shoulders

soon they will call it a night and go back
to their own muteness out of range

IN THE MORNING

morning breaks as a white horse
throws her shadow
in the spray of the waves on the beach
ahead   her traces in the sand

in the afternoon a red horse
flicks her shadow
in the glittering mouth of the river
an invisible shape drinking water

evening falls as a chestnut horse
casts her shadow
in the cool breeze blowing across the grass
the thick legs of a grasshopper crossing the universe

    what's left as night fades
    the shadow
    of one cantering mare
    the sun on her back

        the earth is always
        only half bright
        four-legged wind

TIME PASSES

at the platform after the train left
a notebook on a bench that no one opens
a dried out rose bush that no longer needs water
a bike left unlocked

at the crossing after the train left
a pair of shoes
a tread-worn tire
a dog collar bearing no name

on the beach after the train left
a philosophical tome
a corroded bench
a steel pot   a tatami mat   and a roof

after the train left
a cat's loneliness and a dog's absurdity
a monkey's despair and a bird's desire
and my birth

it was not actually a train
but a school of dolphins
a pride lions
fairies   sprites   and all sorts of others

NOT IMPLICIT

I'm the cage   within which a bird disappeared
tiny and ever flitting
flapping   hopping
until one day   suddenly   the bird trembled and died

its silhouette   erased
the wind shifted   and since then
I haven't felt the same   there's something
concealed   that keeps hovering around me

      depleted   that's the feeling
      I'm a hollow cage
      when I see wings and tiny little legs
        I imagine us   together   in the boundless sky

sometimes   I can hear   a bird singing
start to sense   a twittering
a fluttering
I am again

looming over this   violently   emptied   room

JANUARY 1, 2021

late December at sunset   combing Soma beach
I picked up a spiral shell
now it's dawn   New Year's Day

   without warning the tide rose
   with an eerie stillness

   soon it was higher than 9 meters
   a pitch dark monster wave
   life   and death   and tears   and fish

   and wind   and boats   and cars

   and downed electric poles

   the nuclear power plants failed on the twelfth and fourteenth
      of March 2011

   scores of people evacuated

   the sea called my name
   frightened
   I pretended not to hear

   can time crash over us in waves?

   did I really not hear?

   in its spiral   can a seashell hold

a decade of memories
in the palm of my hand
I felt a chill

      *

"more shaking. such big tremors.
we've continued to expect big aftershocks
and now it seems like we're in it again."

      (3/16/2011)

      *

ahhhh
quaking
still now
we live
day by day

      *

"a missing person becomes a valid missing person
after a report is filed. without a report
they cannot be a valid missing person.
so, is a missing person a missing person?"

      (3/16/2011)

JANUARY 7, 2021

I swooned
reeled
reeling.

it was spring, one year after the disaster.
I boarded a helicopter and traveled into the restricted zone,
the 20 km surrounding the nuclear power station,
high above, looking over the land below.

from a perfectly kept beach,
we crossed into the forbidden sky,
as though we were trespassing.

the land left just as it was that day.

    huge, concrete wave-breaks strewn on the beach.
    houses, cars, and boats hit by the tsunami, scattered everywhere.
    mud and stones spread across roads and fields, electric poles keeled over.
    dogs chained at front doors and left behind ...

time stopped.

no. time doesn't exist.

I remembered that.

dizzy. still now.

could be. the aftershocks.

which continue even now, I think.

the other day, I heard a story

from a dairy farmer living within 20 km of the power station.

"the cows were so hungry

there were teeth marks all through the barn and along the fences.

until the end, trying to find something to eat.

they wasted to skin and bones then fell over…"

*

"tomorrow, what will you be doing? tomorrow, like today, getting by. an aftershock.

tomorrow, what will you be doing? tomorrow, like today, standing here. an aftershock.

a local broadcaster says, now everyone has heard of Fukushima. if we can recover, it's an opportunity for us, he says. we're known all over the world. an aftershock.

we clung to hope. tried to be grateful. is there a reward? maybe. but.
our families and our roots are here. famous around the world? I'll burn the map.

an aftershock.

it's calm. the night air, radiation. an aftershock."

(March 22, 2011)

JANUARY 10, 2021

every

ripe persimmon
left untouched
and soon to fall

winter, the year of the disaster
in these now wild fields
turning red, past ripe
as if burning on the boughs
falling one after another

so
but
still

branches as skeletons
in the sky
hanging down
getting heavier
this whole time
more orange, more red
ripening

left behind
untouched
for ten years

in midair

is it sweet?

is it bitter?

*

"in a quiet moment, when I try to understand

the meaning of this catastrophe, when I try to see it clearly

there's nothing, it's meaningless

something close to darkness, that's all."

(3/16/2011)

JANUARY 11, 2021

what springs to mind this morning
is that blue and orange
big catch flag
lost from a fishing boat

after the tsunami   I found the flag in the beach dunes
twisted in a heap
and carefully spread it out on the sand

that's the memory
examining the flag

it was the first time that I'd looked at one upclose
they are beautiful   really

    then the tragedy and regret set in
    my mind whispers
    it's impossible now
    to have a good catch

        *

spring   seven years later
a fisherman named Haruo Ono in the town of Shinchi
built and launched a new boat
he took me out on it
his brother was washed away in the tsunami
so he gave this new boat the name
of what had been his brother's boat

clear skies ahead   setting out on this first voyage
a brand-new fisherman's flag with clouds and wind, fluttering

we made a circle through the water
as a prayer to the spirits
cut a crisp line back into the harbor
to a waiting crowd

they were cheering
they were clapping
they were waving their hands
they were crying

we waved back at them
from a calm and shining ocean
those of us
still alive

*

"Shining. Calm waves.

On the shore. A seashell.

If I pick it up. It's as though nothing happened.

The world goes back to how it was before.

I pick it up, and ah! just like that, the sunlight and the clouds

the shell in my hand, waiting for this.

Oh force of life, heavier than this earth.

For seashells,

for sunlight, for clouds,

for cows, for train stations, for towns,

for boats, for me.

Even compared to this planet, the force of life."

(4/24/2011)

ACTIVISM AND POETRY: A CONVERSATION WITH BRENDA HILLMAN AND WAGO RYOICHI

Conducted on January 3, 2019 by Ayako Takahashi and Judy Halebsky at Brenda Hillman's home in the East Bay Hills near San Francisco, California, USA.

Halebsky: You are both poets who also teach, what is the role of the poet teacher?

Wago: For me, I started writing poetry at the same time as I started teaching. Teaching helped me realize a lot of things. Much of what I learned through teaching connects directly to writing poetry. When I teach, I try to explain things in a way that my students can best understand. Sometimes I use gestures. With children, I try to think from their point of view and to share the same feelings as them. I focus on building a connection and using direct expression, which is also what I want to do in poetry. It is as if teaching can polish and refine the words in my poems. It's very important to feel with the students and connect my words and feelings with theirs. Teaching and poetry writing are interconnected. Often teaching gives me new insights into my poems.

Hillman: Very close. I feel the same. But I'm very introverted so when I write my poetry, I'm in my very strange dream world. The world inside and the world of my brain and imagination are very separate from that outer practical world. When I go to school and talk to my students about this act of transformation, it always seems like it's a translation of the inner metaphorical universe that's very deep inside of me. Because some of my poetry is very political, I see my teaching as a bridge between these inner metaphoric states of the poet, and the outside world which is sometimes very numb to poetry and art. So my students and the classroom are the bridge into the outside world that doesn't love poetry as much as I do. Very often, I feel like a pagan witch celebrating these magical places of the soul and trying to talk people into my spirit, my world of belief. As a result, I give very easy grades because I want them to like poetry ... So that's my connection. It's a very weird inner world and trying to sell them on it.

Halebsky: So one of the things about teaching being political is that as a poet, you go from a metaphorical state, the internal world of poet, and there's kind of traversing to the outside world. Crossing that bridge is like teaching, and also the political work, or addressing political injustice is also a kind of crossing that bridge.

Hillman: It comes back and forth. The poet is really the transition figure because you're bringing in political things also, especially as an activist poet. Like with Wago's poetry, this disaster happens to you and you have to bring it into relationship to meaning, the world of meaning. Your poetry is full of questions like the ones I was reading where you're asking, *is there someone who is important to you?* There are situations where you might lose them in an instant. If you just think about that for a minute, you realize the only thing you can do is risk your whole being so the world does not rip them away. Mostly the poet has to think that way. It's powerful because you have access to the language and the metaphor that most people don't.

Wago: When I went to Korea in the summer of 2017, poets discussed many things, such as catastrophe, and tragic events around the world.

A huge concern was the ferry that sank while carrying high school students on a field trip. They haven't yet recovered the ferry or the remains. I realized that many people are suffering from different kinds of catastrophes in each country, in all places.

Hillman: Yes, we are under a sense of catastrophe, like with Fukushima obviously, but it's not as focused on one event. In California, we have wildfires now relating to climate change that are so immediate and terrifying. I think about it every day. It feels like we are living in a time of impending disaster. It's not just political, it's climate change or earthquakes. So back to our earlier question, how does the poet translate in a time of disaster across the inner world to the outer world, or from the outer world to the inner world?

Takahashi: To transform that to and from catastrophe.

Hillman: Yes. As you did with your poems where you're taking the moment of your consciousness. You ask, what meaning could there be in harming us to this extent? The meaning of all things is probably determined after the fact. If so, then what is the meaning of that period after the fact? Where you say, *is there any meaning there at all*? You know, at what point in the tragedy is the poet finding meaning? After the fact?

Wago: The tsunami came, my students' families died. That's the first fact. Fukushima Daiichi Power Station was in meltdown, our town was lost and all the people living there were evacuating. That's the second fact. These two facts were overlapping. These things happened at the same time and overlapped. The fact was so big that I tried to live to solve what it meant. It was a tremendous accident, confronting this event, I felt that meaning was disappearing and that the opposite of meaning, no-meaning, was coming closer to what I experienced. I mentioned this in what I wrote during the aftershocks. Another is that I've been practicing "automatism" in my writing practice since I was twenty years old. I've been keeping up with this style of writing from the unconscious ever since. So, my writing is likely to be abstract or to have no-meaning rather than a clear message. My poetry is written by intuition. My poems are complete when I have a feeling of not being myself, when I am someone writing with an enthusiastic mind. I wrote a series of poems as tweets during and following 3.11 [the Tōhoku Earthquake and Tsunami]. When I was swinging in the earthquake, I wrote by intuition and without thinking ... Morning is the entrance to our ordinary life and a time when I can easily get into automatic writing. That's why I wake up at 4am, even though I am tired and will I have to go to work later. When I wake up at 4 or 5 in the morning, amorphous thoughts are floating around me. I can sense things that do not readily form into images or words. On the other hand, in the evening and at night, what I come up with is somehow ordinary.

Hillman: Is there such a thing as ecopoetics in Japan? Is that a very big thing?

Takahashi: Not yet in Japan. We have long standing poetry forms, such as Haiku and Tanka, that are very close to nature and are written through a process of sketching or sketch-writing from nature and the mind at the same time. Still today, Tanka and Haiku are largely written this way. Free verse poetry is one of the major movements in contemporary Japanese poetry. It is largely subject oriented, mind oriented. I would also include visual poetry in this group. In Japan, we have an awareness of the haiku mind, being attuned to the natural world, and the poetry of that world surrounding us. We think of nature as very close to us physically and emotionally. Nature doesn't mean wilderness but something we call *satoyama*. It's the co-existence of nature in urban areas, the seminatural spaces within and beside populated areas. There is a long standing concern to be respectful of nature as well as these seminatural spaces but since Hiroshima and Nagasaki and the toxic contamination of the bombings, there has been an awareness and concern for pollution. There is a body of literature sensitive to pollution and contamination, sometimes called Toxic Discourse. But compared to contemporary poetry in the United States, the poems are less likely to be sensitive to social injustice or gender roles or race. Many women do not realize that their problems are really connected to social injustice. Many Japanese people do not have this awareness. Does that make sense?

Hillman: Makes sense. Yes. And you know, in American poetry now, it's coming together, at least I'm aware in my own poetry that it's coming together. When they ask me why are you writing ecopoetics, what is this? I say, well I came from a romantic nature tradition, to modernism then to postmodernism. I think of ecopoetics as worried nature poetry. That's my definition. You can't really go out into nature and feel safe anymore. So it's not easy to define one's self as a romantic poet anymore. You're worried, you know, about climate change. [My poem] "Crypto-animist Introvert Activism" is an ecopoem because it brings together the consciousness of social justice and also that there is a realm of nature very close by. I believe in the spirit world. I talk to my ancestors and the other spirits and dead poets. So I have a sense that you can write about social justice and nature and ecopoetics and have this interior space all at the same time. I think that is what is happening in American poetry now. In Japan, is there worry about the environment as much as there is in America, do you think? I mean before Fukushima?

Wago: Though Japan is a narrow island country, some people are not as keenly aware of environmental problems, including environmental destruction and pollution. Actually it's very difficult to solve the fundamental problems that cause environmental degradation. First, we need to separate these problems into three types: community, national, and worldwide. When I was an undergraduate student, Professor Masahiro Sawa said to me, "a poet is not a true poet unless they have the power to make change in their environment." Here "environment" includes both the natural world and the environment that surrounds natural and human spaces, including human activity. In terms of ecopoetry, poems have the power and ability to transform without stating directly. At the same time, if direct, straight and descriptive expressions are written as poems, they have the power to deliver fresh messages.

Halebsky: Considering social protest, political protest and poetry, how are they connected? Is there a social role for poetry? Does poetry have a social responsibility?

Wago: Yes, yes. One of my poems has the lines, "to live in Fukushima, to live Fukushima." affirming that life in Fukushima-city means to be part of the evolving story of this place, for better or worse. This sentiment resonated with many people. They heard these words and were drawn back to Fukushima. A section from one of my poems was sung as part of a protest at the National Government Council against the changing of the constitution. Historically, Japanese poetry tends not to focus on epic stories with a social or historical aspect. I experienced this catastrophe and lived through a time when reality transcended what we know to be ordinary, I lived through a hyper reality. Through this experience, I came to write ordinary life as it is. That is the record of my poetry. It is a document and record of a mind epic. I was able to share the regularity of the catastrophe through live reports by live broadcasting through social media. What I was able to witness, report and deliver to an audience of readers led to social protest and political protest.

Hillman: I've done a lot of political activism. After the Iraq War, people began asking me about the role of poetry in social justice or political justice activism and how the two are related. One is that as an activist, I used to think they had nothing to do with each other. Like this, when I was in my room and I was a private strange person, like we were talking about in the beginning, I thought this private strange Brenda has nothing to do with the activist person who goes to Congress or whatever. Then I began to think, yes they do, they come together a lot, because you always bring your strange interior self into the city, surrounded by other people. You're always bringing your imagination into the street if you're protesting. But that's very different from thinking that poetry will make change. I'm in a little disagreement with [Professor Sawa's] teaching that you read because I think poetry doesn't cause the change, I think poetry accompanies the change. I have a friend who wrote a really wonderful sentence I thought a lot about. He said, 'poetry is not the riot, it's the riot dog'. It's the dog running alongside of the protest. And I like that sentence because that's exactly how I feel. I always have a poem in my pocket when I'm out on the street protesting.

I've given up on the government more or less. I used to go to Congress a lot and try to talk them out of bombing Iraq. Every few weeks I would fly to Washington D.C. and I would be trying to talk them out of the bombing. I would go into the Congressional offices, and I would take a political poem or whatever. I realized this isn't going to make a difference. What helps is to know that intelligent and sensitive people are out in the world doing this work. I still believe that doing local legislation and protest are very important, and poets are not exempt from doing this. I don't know if that's true in Japan. We can't be so sensitive that we only stay in our room and write.

I think with Twitter, with the poetry you've been writing, it is a way of getting it out to many more people. But I also think with poets, like I say to myself, one day a week I have to be doing political work besides poetry, because poetry can't make all the changes. It's very uncomfortable now in the era of Trump. I know poets do not want to be near Trump. Poets were fine being near Obama, he was a reader. I have a lot to say on this subject because I have done so many political activities and I think it's limited. Poets are absolutely essential for the universe, but we can't expect poetry to be changing climate change legislation. It's not going to happen.

Halebsky: I feel like one of the things poetry can do is nourish our compassion. A hardened person engaging in poetry can soften in such a way that they become compassionate for the animals, for the environment, for people's sufferings. I think that's one of the ways poetry works almost politically.

Hillman: But the problem is a lot of people think poetry has a different kind of power than it does, because they are thinking about polemicals... Wago's poetry is a testimonial to what he experienced. It's not going to change legislation or your government or make Trump sign the Paris Peace Accord. It's not going to happen, but it can change hearts, it's true. I've seen people change their political views a little bit when they start writing poetry. But mostly it's like they start writing poetry because they're already wise and compassionate.

Halebsky: Or it keeps them on a compassionate path.

Hillman: Exactly. I'm not cynical about it, but I just feel poetry, it's the riot dog, it's not the riot. It's the one running beside. It's what you put in your pocket. It's not going to change the legislation. For that we have to work in a different way. And mostly poets are just so sensitive. When I was going to Washington people would say, oh you're going to Washington, what are you doing there? I would say,

I'm a teacher, I'm a grandmother, I'm going into these offices and I'm saying, stop fighting, stop the war, and there's just these little kids sitting at the desks. I would hand them the facts, or I would hand them the poems, and I would say, I flew from California with my own money to tell you I'm very upset about this. But I was the same as any other grandmother when I did that. I didn't have any special power.

Halebsky: How can poetry support, propel environmental consciousness?

Hillman: That is easier I think. It is way easier because of social media. There's a lot on social media that the kids, the students and the young people are very easily swayed by poetry, if you make it sexy, you know? I teach the ecopoetics class and they love this class. The business majors, the biologists, all of the students love taking the ecopoetics class because we go outside and we talk about how if they're engaged with nature, then they can help save it. That's much easier than the whole question of whether poetry has political power. Because of course you can raise consciousness of the environment with kids and everyone. We can do it in one week. The business majors, they're ready to sign up for life. They start writing poetry and they go, *oh*!

Wago: Kenji Miyazawa was a celebrated poet and writer of children's literature. Born in 1896, he lived in a small town in the Tōhoku area for almost all of his life. After his death, his work became popular. It expresses ordinary life in his small town at a time when there was growing awareness about Europe and Europe's history and culture. Sometimes he would change ordinary Japanese names into fictional names. He was prolific and wrote a lot of children's literature. He changed the name of his poor hometown, from Hanamaki, Iwate to Ihatov, a made up word that he imaged to mean a paradise. His work has brought attention to his hometown and still today many people visit Hanamaki. He wrote, "If all people aren't happy, I cannot be happy." "The reality where we live is the true art itself." "Let's build society to protect poor or weak people." His ideas speak for many people from children to elders. Like Kenji, I still think that poetry has the power to change the environment and the individual. I'd like to be this kind of writer, a poet who can change not only our environment but the individual.

Hillman: That's so interesting. About teaching, one of the most important things that poet teachers and poet activists can do is to show that everything is related, that everything is connected. It's not just about your own little system, or your own little country, or your own little family, it's all connected. It's also connected to the invisible world, everything inside of our bodies, we can't see it, but it's connected, it's connected to the climate. So poets do have a very important spiritual message that we're teaching. Not just compassion but it's also not just you as lonely as you feel and as terrified as you are, it's not just you by yourself, you're connected to the whole world.

Takahashi: That's a kind of ecopoetics.

Hillman: That's the main thing about ecopoetics. It's about the world as a web. Everything is interrelated, and the inter-relationships are what we study. That's why there's a lot of interesting poetry that's connecting these things. To me that's the main point.

Takahashi: Connecting, transcending time, like transcending space.

Hillman: Yes, across, deeper, outer, inner, you know. If you use a chemical on this piece of fruit to make this a nice orange, it affects everything. It's not just one thing. It's everything together. That's the main message poetry can bring. This comes back to where we started with the classroom.

Wago: Since the Fukushima meltdown, I've been asking myself what I should I write as a poet. I'd like to write about nature. Not nature worldwide, not globally, but locally. About nature as it is where I live in Fukushima. Like Henry David Thoreau's *Walden*, he wrote about the small world right in front of him but was able to reach beyond that to touch on shared concerns, even transcendent things. For me, after the catastrophe, everything was ruthlessly lost. I was bereft. Even after radioactive contamination, there's still a living land, rivers, oceans, trees, animals, and so on. I'd like to write about how we face such a stricken land, how we face Fukushima as it is. Every time I thought about writing, about nature or wilderness, my mind came to American poetry, nature poets or protesting poets. And that I have a responsibility as a poet. There are three aspects of writing poetry: past, present, and future. For the past, I am inspired by the accomplishments of previous poets. For the present, I try to face social reality as it is and express it as clearly as possible in an understandable way by facing that reality directly. And finally the future, I try to show a new generation what we have aspired to, the work their parents have done and do now. I'll teach children how important it is that they think for themselves, engage with society, face our shared struggles.

ACKNOWLEDGMENTS

Our work translating these poems has been generously supported by the Japanese Society for the Promotion of Science (JSPS). Thanks also Keetje Kuipers at *Poetry Northwest*, to Emily Wolahan and Sarah Coolidge at *Two Lines* for being enthusiastic about these translations and giving them a place to live in the world, and the team at *Tokyo Poetry Journal*. This book had many readers who offered immensely helpful comments and ideas, particularly Shigeyoshi Hara, Anne Pelletier, Alexa Weinstein, and Jaime Libby. Forrest Gander was generous in his feedback and guidance. Brenda Hillman and Robert Hass welcomed us to their home. Hillman spent many hours in a biligual discussion of ecopoetry with Wago. Jane Hirshfield has offerd her ongoing generous advice. Eliot Weinberger also kindly offered us guidance. Thanks also to the poets and translators at the Napa Valley Writers Conference and the Ensenada Avenue Poets.

Two Lines: "In the Flesh of Peach" "Ghosts" "January 10, 2021" "January 11, 2021" and "Thoughts of the Abandoned".

Poetry Northwest: "Blown by the Wind" "Evacuation" "Suffering" "Screening" (now titled 'Screening Notes') "12 Plastic Bottles" (now titled 12 Bottles) and "QQQ".

Tokyo Poetry Journal: "A Short Life" "Post-Fukushima Interview #6" "Abandoned Fukushima" "Out of Range" and "January 1, 2021".

NOTES

Pebbles of Poetry Part 1 and 9. This text is excerpted from tweets that Wago posted starting five days after the earthquake on March 16, 2011 at 4:23 am.

In the Flesh of a Peach. This poems names the 'contamination zone' which is a 20 km area directly surrounding the Fukushima Daiichi Nuclear Power Plant. No one is permitted to enter the area nor are airplanes permitted to fly over the area. This poem along with *A Short Life* and *Post-Fukushima Interview #6* were originally published in 2011 in a collection titled *Running Into Poetry*.

Post-Fukushima Interview #6. 150 years ago, the town Aizuwakamatsu was the site of a battle during a civil war, known as the Boshin war. The Aizu defeated the government army and people in this area fled for their lives. A Japanese readership would quickly recognize the significance of the place name, Aizuwakamatsu. It is now a tourist area with a museum that tells the history of the area.

Evacuation, Suffering, Screening Notes, Screening Time, and *You* are excerpted from a book-length series titled "Remembering Spring: Disaster Notes" These poems were written after Wago visited the town of Namie, which is within 20 km of the failed nuclear power plant. This collection along with *Pebbles of Poetry* are inspired by the modern Japanese poet, Chuya Nakahara. Lines from his poems written in the 1930s include, "Oh, it's still and calm. Oh, coming around, this is my upcoming spring" and "for all the past, tears spring out. The walls of the castle have dried / a wind blows". When Wago entered Namie, wearing a hazmat suit, he saw the town completely abandoned. But he also saw that birds were flying, salmon were swimming upriver, and persimmons were in fruit. He found that despite the huge disruption and loss of life for so many, there were other lives continuing like the wind in Chuya's poem.

"U.S. Art Museums Cancel The Fukushima Leg Of Ben Shahn's Traveling Exhibition In Japan" The title of this poem is from a newspaper headline that ran in February, 2012. Wago was greatly disturbed by the decision of U.S. Art Museums to cancel a planned exhibit in Fukushima. At a moment of such trauma, loss and devastation, these museums refused to send artwork to the area which might have offered solace to the community. Ben Shahn is a 20th century U.S. artist known for work that addresses war, poverty and discrimination. Shahn's paintings and photographs are part of the permanent collection of the Fukushima Prefectural Museum of Art. Wago saw Shahn's work on exhibit at the museum and felt a deep connection to the themes and approach of the images. Wago explains that news of the canceling of this exhibition provoked in him a moment of absolute clarity that was a catalyst for him to resume his writing and activism on behalf of the people of Fukushima. In response, Wago wrote new posts on Twitter and new poems.

Spring & Thorn. This poem is inspired by Sakutarou Hagiwara's poem "Sentimental Fingers" from *Barking to the Moon* (1917). In Hagiwara's poem, he writes, "sad for thousands of hands/ hands are always over our heads" lamenting summers and falls when he played the Chinese fiddle. Now his fingers have turned to lead. It continues, "Finally, these hands dig into rich soil, connecting with the dirt, getting thorns from spring flowers". This poem along with *Thoughts of the Abandoned* and *Abandoned Fukushima* were originally published in *Book of Decommisioned Poem* (2013).

Thoughts of the Abandoned. This poem is based on tweets Wago posted on March 27, 2011 in the weeks following the nuclear meltdown (see

Pebble of Poetry, Part 9). The poem uses the scientific term *rinkai* to refer to nuclear criticality. Nuclear reactors generate power by establishing a fission chain reaction. Criticality is when the nuclear plant creates an ongoing chain reaction that is controlled and sustained. A nuclear meltdown occurs when the mechanisms to control that reaction fail. We have translated criticality as a "self-sustaining nuclear chain reaction".

Ghosts. This poem begins with *withered fields* which is a reference to one of Basho's last haiku, *Ill on a journey/ my dreams still wandering/over withered fields* (旅に病んで夢は枯野をかけ廻る). This brings a sense of death and the fragility of life to the opening of the poem. Much of the description in the poem addresses efforts to lower radiation levels near Fukushima Daiichi Nuclear Power Plant. One method is to collect the topsoil which is now contaminated with radioactive pollution in large bags. These bags are then piled into deeper holes dug in the ground and buried. The poem also references the novella *Salamander* by Masuji Ibuse (1898-1993). It is a story about a salamander that lives in a cave for two years. One day a frog comes into the cave. The frog's freedom to come and go reveals to the salamander that he himself is trapped in the cave. This poems along with *Abandoned Room, Blown by the Wind, 12 Bottles, Family, QQQ,* and *Out of Range* were originally published in the collection *QQQ* in 2018.

Q Q Q. The meltdown of Fukushima Daiichi Power Plant forced people living within 20 km to evacuate. There were more than three hundred farming families in the area and three thousand cows, pigs and hens were left behind.

In the Morning, Time Passes, and *Not Implicit.* These poems were written in Japanese but have English language titles. "In the Morning" and "Time Passes" are the original titles of these poems as they were published in Japanese. For the English translation of the poem "Not Implicit" we adjusted the original title which was "No Implicitly". These poems are from the collection *Transit* published in 2021.

January 1, January 7, January 10, and *January 11, 2021*. Starting on New Year's Day in 2011, Wago wrote a poem each day for eleven days remembering the disaster ten years earlier. Each poem adds context to a Twitter post Wago wrote during the first days of the nuclear meltdown in March, 2011. The original tweet is quoted directly in each poem and includes the date it was posted to Twitter. These poems are part of the book, *Envisioning the Future: Pebbles of Poetry 10 Years Later*, published in 2011. They appear in a section of that book titled, *Seashell Poetry – Book of Remembering the Fukushima Disaster*.

SOURCES

Hatsuzawa, Toshio, and Takehito Takano. "Characteristics of the Evacuation Area and the Spatial Distribution of Radioactive Pollution in Fukushima Prefecture." *Japan after 3/11: Global Perspectives on the Earthquake, Tsunami, and Fukushima Meltdown*, edited by Pradyumna P. Karan and Unryu Suganuma, University Press of Kentucky, 2016.

Karan, Pradyumna P. "Introduction.: After the Triple Disaster: Landscape of Devastation, Despair, Hope, and Resilience." *Japan after 3/11: Global Perspectives on the Earthquake, Tsunami, and Fukushima Meltdown*, edited by Pradyumna P. Karan and Unryu Suganuma, University Press of Kentucky, 2016.

Seki, Reiko. "Deprivation of Hometown: Evacuees 10 Years After the Fukushima Nuclear Power Plant Accident" Center for Japanese Studies, University of California Berkeley. 28 April 2021. Zoom Lecture. (Written lecture and slides shared later via email correspondence).

Wago, Ryoichi. *Pebbles of Poetry (Shi no Tsubute)*. Tokyo, Tokuma Press, 2011.
---. *Running into Poetry (Shi no Kaikou)*. Tokyo: Asahi Press, 2011.
---. *Pebbles of Poetry, Volume 2 (Shi no Tsubute 2)*. Tokyo: Tokuma Press, 2012.
---. *What Comes Out In Words: After the Tōhoku Earthquake, Tsunami and Nuclear Meltdown (Kotoba ni Nani ga Dekirunoka: 3.11 wo Koete)*. Tokyo, Tokuma, 2012.
---. *Remembering Spring: Disaster Notes 2011/03/11-2012/03/11, (Futatabi no Harui ni)*. Tokyo: Shodensha Press, 2012.

---. *Decommissioned Poetry (Hairoshihen)*. Tokyo: Shichosha Press, 2013.
---. *QQQ*. Tokyo: Shichosha Press, 2018.
---. *Selected Poems (Zoku Wago Ryoichi Shishu)*. Contemporary Poets Series. Tokyo: Shichosha Press, 2018.
---. *Transit*. Tokyo: Nanarokusha Press, 2021.
---. *Envisioning the Future: Pebbles of Poetry 10 Years Later (Mirai Taru Shi no Tsubete Jyuunenki)*. Tokyo: Tokuma Press, 2021.

About the author

Wago Ryoichi is a poet and high school Japanese literature teacher from Fukushima City, Japan. In 2017, the French translation of his book *Pebbles of Poetry* won the Nunc Magazine award for best foreign-language poetry collection. Wago has published many solo author volumes of poetry. Since March 2011, his writing has focused on the ecological devastation of the areas affected by the Tōhoku earthquake, tsunami and the nuclear meltdown of the Fukushima Daiichi power station. His poem *Abandoned Fukushima* is sung by choirs across Japan as a prayer for hope and renewal.

About the translators

Takahashi Ayako and Judy Halebsky work collaboratively to translate poetry between English and Japanese. Takahashi Ayako is a scholar and translator teaching at University of Hyogo in Japan. Her recent scholarship includes the books *Ambience: Ecopoetics in the Anthropocene* (Shichosha, 2022) and *Reading Gary Snyder* (Shichosha 2018). She has published translations of many American poets such as Jane Hirshfield, Anne Waldman, and Joanne Kyger, among others (*Anthology of Contemporary American Women Poets*, Shichosha Press 2012). Judy Halebsky is a poet and translator. She is the author of *Spring and a Thousand Years (Unabridged)* (University of Arkansas Press, 2020), *Tree Line* (New Issues 2014) and *Sky=Empty*, winner of the New Issue Prize (New Issues, 2010). She has also published articles on cultural translation and noh theatre. She is a professor of Literature and Language and director of the MFA in Creative Writing program at Dominican University of California. Ayako and Judy have been working together for a number of years and have previously published articles in Japan on the development of English language haiku.

www.ingramcontent.com/pod-product-compliance
Lightning Source LLC
Chambersburg PA
CBHW031405160426
43196CB00007B/908